THE GREAT PANDA TALE

CITY
ZOO

Admits one

Issue date :

By Laura Buller

LONDON, NEW YORK, MUNICH,
MELBOURNE, AND DELHI

DK LONDON
Series Editor Deborah Lock
Project Editor Camilla Gersh
Project Art Editor Hoa Luc
Production Editor Francesca Wardell

Reading Consultant Shirley Bickler

DK DELHI
Editor Nandini Gupta
Assistant Art Editor Yamini Panwar
DTP Designer Anita Yadav
Picture Researcher Aditya Katyal
Deputy Managing Editor Soma B. Chowdhury
Design Consultant Shefali Upadhyay

First published in Great Britain by
Dorling Kindersley Limited
80 Strand, London, WC2R 0RL

Copyright © 2014 Dorling Kindersley Limited
A Penguin Company

10 9 8 7 6 5 4 3 2 1
001—196474—January/2014

A CIP catalogue record for this book
is available from the British Library.

ISBN: 978-1-40934-119-2

Printed and bound in China by South China Printing Company.

The publisher would like to thank the following for their kind permission to reproduce their photographs:
(Key: a-above; b-below/bottom; c-centre; f-far; l-left; r-right; t-top)
6 Dreamstime.com: Geopappas (tl / clip). **Pearson Asset Library:** Jon Barlow / Pearson Education Ltd (tl). **8 Corbis:**
Minden Pictures / ZSSD (cb). **9 Corbis:** Minden Pictures / ZSSD (cra). **Pearson Asset Library:** Jon Barlow /
Pearson Education Ltd (clb). **10 Getty Images:** Lonely Planet Images / Richard Nebesky (c). **11 Corbis:**
Imaginechina (c). **12 Dreamstime.com:** Am Wu (bl). **Getty Images:** Photographer's Choice RF / Frank Krahmer
(cla). **13 Getty Images:** AFP / Roslan Rahman (c). **14 Corbis:** Karen Kasmauski (c). **16-17 Getty Images:** AFP /
Alain Jocard (b). **19 Corbis:** Pallava Bagla (t). **20 Corbis:** Minden Pictures / Konrad Wothe (br). **21 Corbis:**
Minden Pictures / Katherine Feng (t); Reuters / Adrees Latif (bl). **22 Fotolia:** Eric Isselee (cla, cl). **23 Fotolia:**
Michael Flippo (b). **25 Corbis:** Xinhua Press / Chen Xie (b). **26 Getty Images:** AFP / Ed Jones (t). **27 Corbis:**
Minden Pictures / Katherine Feng (b). **28 Corbis:** Imaginechina (t). **29 Corbis:** Reuters / San Diego Zoo / Ken
Bohn (c). **30 Corbis:** Xinhua Press / U.S. National Zoo (cl, crb, b). **31 Corbis:** Xinhua Press / U.S. National Zoo
(cl, crb, bl). **33 Corbis:** Reuters. **34 Fotolia:** shama65 (bl). **Getty Images:** Photographer's Choice RF / Frank
Krahmer (cla). **36 Corbis:** Minden Pictures / Katherine Feng (b). **37 Corbis:** Minden Pictures / Katherine Feng (cr).
Getty Images: China Photos (tl). **38 Getty Images:** Asahi Shimbun (b). **39 Dreamstime.com:** Christophe Testi
(tr). **40 Corbis:** Imaginechina (c); Keren Su (tr); Frank Lukasseck (cb). **41 Corbis:** Sandy Huffaker (cb); Reuters /
China Daily (cla); Minden Pictures / JH Editorial / Cyril Ruoso (ca). **42 Getty Images:** Stringer / China Photos (c).
43 Getty Images: ChinaFotoPress (cb). **44 Fotolia:** Eric Isselee (bl, bc). **45 Dreamstime.com:** Eric Isselee (br).
Fotolia: Eric Isselee (bl, cr). **46 Corbis:** Minden Pictures / ZSSD (b). **47 Dreamstime.com:** Roman Milert (t).
48 Fotolia: Eric Isselee (clb); Valeriy Kalyuzhnyy / StarJumper (bl). **49 Getty Images:** Lintao Zhang (b).
50 Getty Images: Jeff J Mitchell (c). **51 Getty Images:** Jeff J Mitchell (t). **52 Dreamstime.com:** Inga Dudkina
(cr, c); Eutoch (cl). **54 Corbis:** Redlink / Min Shan (b). **55 Getty Images:** ChinaFotoPress. **56 Getty Images:** Win
McNamee (cb). **58 Fotolia:** Eric Isselee (cb). **Getty Images:** a.collectionRF / twinmist (ca). **58-59 Corbis:** Minden
Pictures / Katherine Feng. **59 Dreamstime.com:** Isselee (cb). **Getty Images:** China Photos (tl)
Jacket images: Back right: Asahi Shimbun/Getty Images
All others © Dorling Kindersley

All other images © Dorling Kindersley

For further information see: www.dkimages.com

Discover more at
www.dk.com

Contents

Welcome to the Zoo

Step inside the zoo gates. Get ready for an amazing animal adventure!

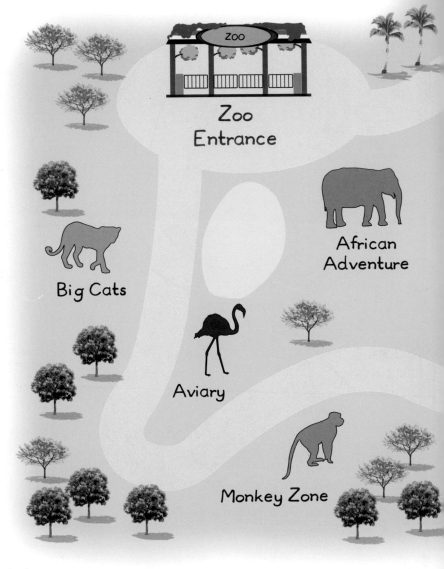

Zoo
Entrance

Big Cats

African
Adventure

Aviary

Monkey Zone

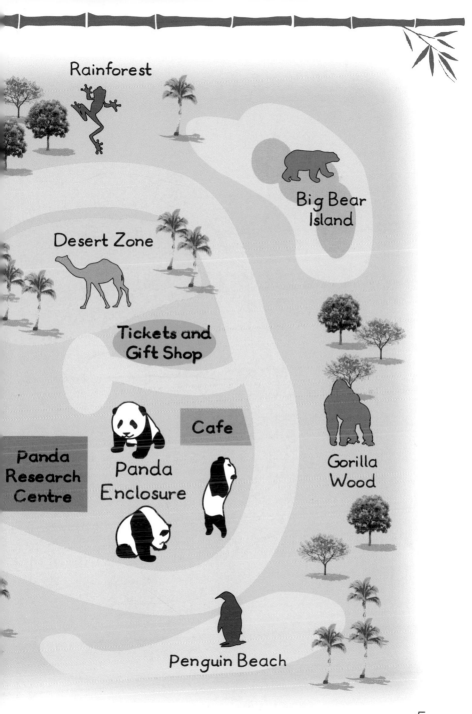

Rainforest

Big Bear
Island

Desert Zone

Tickets and
Gift Shop

Panda
Research
Centre

Cafe

Panda
Enclosure

Gorilla
Wood

Penguin Beach

5

The Great Panda Tale

by Louise Sims

This was our term project: write a story to show and tell something you did this year. Write about a special person or place. Or, tell the story of a big event. You are the star of the story!

Look out for me.
Try saying some
words in Chinese.

Here is my story: I can't wait to tell it!
I had the coolest summer ever. First,
I will tell you what happened. Then, I
will add some little drawings to make
my story more fun. Finally, I will
share my story with the whole class.

Since I was a little girl, the zoo has been my favourite place. I love to learn about all the animals. It is so exciting to see them up close and for real. I love to watch them move and play, and to hear them hoot, growl and roar.

Roarrr!

My family used to tease me. They said I loved the zoo so much, I should move to the monkey house.

Hehe, hehe, hehe!

This year, I did the next best thing. I joined the Zoo Crew. We are kids who help zoo visitors have a great day.

CITY ZOO

Zoo Crew volunteer
Name: Louise
Zoo Crew no. 00123

This is my zoo pass.

Being in the Zoo Crew is so much fun. Every day is different from the last one. Sometimes, we help the zookeepers look after the animals. On busy days, we work at the ticket booth or the gift shop. We never know what to expect!

The busy ticket booth

This summer, something amazing happened. We found out one of our giant pandas was expecting a baby.

It was big news for the zoo, because no panda cubs had ever been born there. This is the story of my best summer ever.

CITY ZOO

Admits one

Issue date :

10 May

Today's shows and talks

 11.30 a.m. Penguin beach talk

 12.00 p.m. Animals in action!

 **12.30 p.m.** Real reptiles!

 **2.00 p.m.** It's a frog's life

Big News at the Zoo

On the day we found out about
the baby, I was taking a package to
the head panda keeper, Ms Kelly.
I walked past the panda enclosure to
the research centre.

The enclosure is so beautiful. It looks
just like the pandas' tree-covered home
in China. I spotted Gao Yun, the male
panda, but Zhen Mei, the female,
was nowhere to be seen.

I could barely open the doors when
I got to the research centre.
The place was packed with people.

Everyone was looking at the big glass
window into the lab. Zhen Mei was
there with two animal doctors.

I was looking too and bumped right
into Ms Kelly. I asked her to tell me
what was going on. She told me
the vets were doing tests on Zhen Mei.
They wanted to find out if she was
going to have a baby.

Ba-Boom!
Ba-Boom!

Say "panda" 熊猫
xióngmāo
(shyong-mow)

People were buzzing with excitement. A few minutes later, one vet held her thumbs up behind the window. A huge cheer went up. A new baby panda was on the way!

This was fantastic news for the whole zoo. Pandas are endangered animals. There are only a few thousand left in the wild. Zoos help pandas to have babies and research how to protect wild pandas.

Panda-monium!
by Lotta Bear

Staff at the City Zoo announced today that giant panda Zhen Mei is expecting a baby.

"We are thrilled to tell everyone our news," said Louise Kelly. Ms Kelly is the Director of Pandas at City Zoo.

This will be the first baby for Zhen Mei, and the first baby panda for City Zoo. There are about 300 giant pandas living in zoos around the world. Zhen Mei and her partner, Gao Yun, came to City Zoo from China five years ago.

A panda mother is pregnant with her baby for three to five months. "We will take extra good care of Zhen Mei," said Ms Kelly. "We can't wait to welcome her baby in the summer."

Visitors to the zoo will still be able to view the panda parents. The new baby will join them in the enclosure when it is four months old.

Panda Habitat

Explore the giant panda's home in the wild.

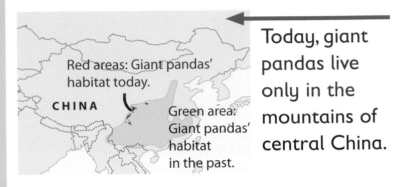

Red areas: Giant pandas' habitat today.

CHINA

Green area: Giant pandas' habitat in the past.

Today, giant pandas live only in the mountains of central China.

Wild pandas live high up in the mountains. The forests are filled with bamboo plants and trees. Pandas shelter from the cold and damp in stone caves or tree dens.

Search 🔍 📷 <u>Panda cam</u>

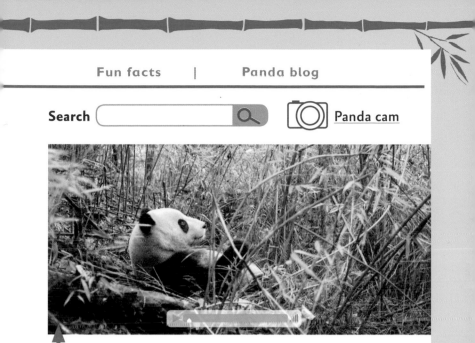

Bamboo is a giant grassy plant. It is a panda's main food.

Pandas are good climbers. They can sleep in trees. Unlike other bears, pandas do not hibernate in winter.

Learn more... >>

21

CITY ZOO

Admits one

Issue date :

17 May

Today's shows and talks

11.00 a.m. Creatures of the night

12.00 p.m. Monkey business

1.00 p.m. Big fish

1.30 p.m. Creepy critters

Getting Ready

Over the next few months, we took extra care with Zhen Mei. My job was to help provide her main meal: bamboo. A panda chews through a huge pile of bamboo every day. Pandas need to eat lots of bamboo to keep healthy.

Panda Menu

Starters

Bamboo leaves
Fruit
Eggs

Vegetarian dishes

(Pandas are meat-eaters but they prefer to eat plants.)
Bamboo leaves
Grass
Carrots

Side dishes

Rice
Insects
Sweet potatoes
Rodents

Seasonal dishes
Spring bamboo shoots
Winter bamboo stems

Kids' menu
Bamboo shoots
(Must be six months old to order.)
Milk
Milk porridge

Desserts
Bamboo leaves
Bamboo biscuits

A panda's long thumb helps it grasp and move the plant.

Its huge jaws crush the bamboo stems.

25

One of the zookeepers
pulling a trolley of
bamboo for the pandas

The zookeepers kept a close eye on
how much Zhen Mei was eating.
They wanted to make sure her baby
was healthy and growing. One vet
did some tests on her poop.
I wouldn't like to have that job!

Zoo workers made the panda enclosure ready for the big day. Zhen Mei needed more time away from the visitors, so they built her a den. They put different toys and playthings in the den to keep Zhen Mei and Gao Yun active and alert.

Around July, we noticed that Zhen Mei was eating less bamboo. She seemed to want to be alone in the den almost all the time. Was it time for the baby to be born? The vets gave her lots of different tests.

Say "today" 今天
jīntiān
(jin-tee-yan)

28

They used an ultrasound machine to see the baby inside her. Afterwards, Ms Kelly told me that Zhen Mei's cubs looked strong and healthy. Cubs! I couldn't believe it. Our panda mum was going to have twins.

An ultrasound is a special picture of a baby while still inside its mother.

Over the next week, Zhen Mei seemed to spend almost all her time in her den. The zoo team watched her on the panda cam, as she snoozed most of the day. The vets thought this was a sign the twins were ready to be born.

Panda cam

10.01 a.m.

12.14 p.m.

1.55 p.m.

Early one morning, the zookeepers heard a strange noise from the panda enclosure. They checked Zhen Mei. They found her with her new cubs. The tiny babies were crying for milk. Soon the news spread through the zoo. The babies were here: a boy and a girl!

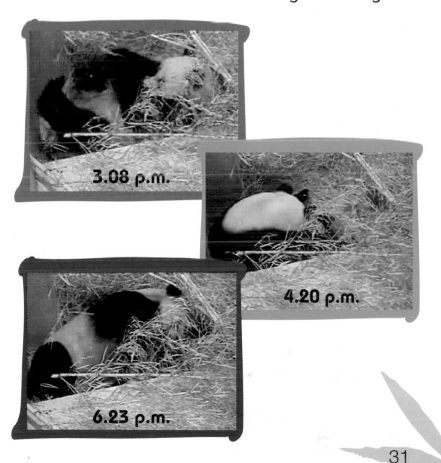

3.08 p.m.

4.20 p.m.

6.23 p.m.

Our New Arrivals!

A boy
born 22 July at 5.39
in the morning
105 grams (4 oz) and
15 centimetres (5 in.)

and a girl
born 22 July at 5.46
in the morning
95 grams (3 oz) and
12 centimetres (4.5 in.)

to the proud parents
Zhen Mei and Gao Yun.

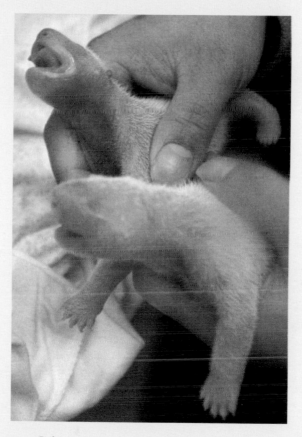

As in Chinese tradition,
the babies will be named
after 100 days.

CITY ZOO

Admits one

Issue date :

22 July

Today's shows and talks

11.30 a.m. Penguin beach talk

12.15 p.m. Babes in the bush

1.00 p.m. Big cat friends

2.30 p.m. Elegant elephants

A Pair of Pandas

The panda cubs were tiny enough to cup in your hands. They were a thousand times smaller than their mother. They were pink and wrinkly, with a few patches of white hair on their bodies. Every two hours, they cried to be fed.

No other mammal has babies so much smaller than the adult. At birth, a panda weighs only 100 grams.

Panda and cub

Cat and kitten

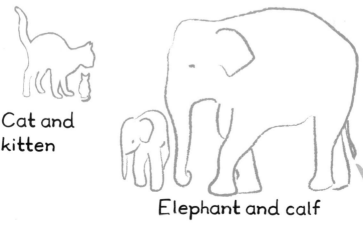

Elephant and calf

The cubs' eyes were squeezed shut.
They spent most of their time
sleeping and feeding. This was just
like me when I was a newborn.
Zhen Mei hardly ever put the babies
down. She cradled them in her big
panda paws. She sometimes
popped one in her mouth.

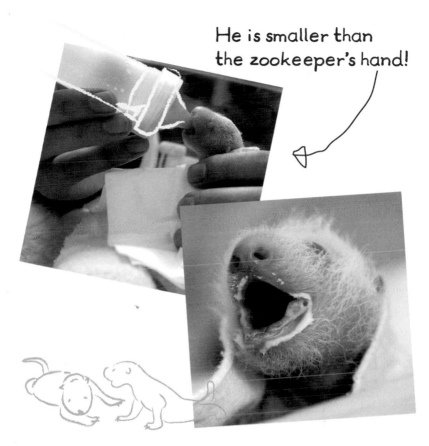

He is smaller than the zookeeper's hand!

The zookeepers made sure both babies were getting enough to eat. They had a lot of growing to do! Each cub drank milk from a bottle. You could see a row of tiny white teeth when they opened their hungry mouths.

The panda twins were nearly six weeks old. I watched them through a glass window in their nursery. They were so cute! They were ten times their birth size. Patches of black fur had grown around their eyes, ears, shoulders and little legs.

Their eyes were open now, too.

Vote for your favourite
panda baby name

Little Cloud ☐

Snowdrop ☐

Sunshine ☐

Tea Cup ☐

The zoo asked everyone to choose
names for the new pandas on
its website. People voted for their
favourites. I really liked the winning
names, Little Cloud for the male
and Snowdrop for the female.

Panda Names

Pandas come from China.
That is why they always
have Chinese names.

My name is
Xuehua. It
means Snowdrop.

My name is Xiao
Yun, which means
Little Cloud.

My name is Zhen
Mei. This means
Beautiful Pearl.

My name is Gao Yun, meaning Big Cloud.

My name is Yang Guang. It means Sunshine.

My name is Xing Xing. It means Stars...

My name is Zhu Zhu, which means Bamboo.

My name is Heping Xiong. This means Peaceful Bear.

41

At two months old, the cubs were crawling and would take their first steps soon. Every week, the vets gave them a checkup. They weighed and measured them to make sure they were growing well. Sometimes the cubs tried to wriggle away.

The vets gave the cubs all kinds of toys at the checkups. It was so much fun to watch them play. Snowdrop really loved her red ball. I didn't think she would ever let go of it. She and her brother had to be the cutest babies in the whole zoo.

Zoo Babies

Snowdrop and Little Cloud are not the only new arrivals. The zoo has lots of babies!

Red pandas are grey when they are first born but turn red as they grow.

Sloth babies cling to their mums for the first few months of their lives.

Newborn giant pandas are very tiny, but they can make a lot of noise!

Baby rhinos are heavy! They can weigh 40-65 kg (88-140 lb) when they are born.

Young orang-utans like to hold hands when they travel through the trees.

A baby gorilla rides on his mum's back when she walks through the jungle.

Little lions and their mums live in groups with other mums and cubs.

Little Cloud and Snowdrop began walking when they were around four months old. Little Cloud could even run for a few steps. Snowdrop sometimes climbed on her mother's back for a ride.

Coming soon: baby pandas!

On show in November.
Baby viewing hours:
11.30 a.m. to 1.00 p.m.

Both cubs followed their mother everywhere. They copied everything she did, from climbing trees to eating bamboo. Soon, it would be time for visitors to see the panda twins.

Say "hello"
nǐ hǎo
(nee how)

你好

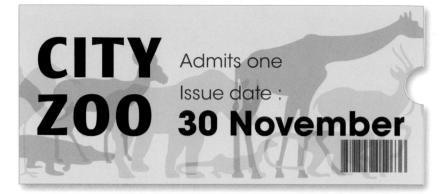

CITY ZOO

Admits one

Issue date :

30 November

Today's shows and talks

10.30 a.m. Seal show

12.00 p.m. Rainforest wonders

2.30 p.m. Koala kids

3.00 p.m. On safari

Pandas on Parade

I remember the day Snowdrop and Little Cloud joined their mother in the enclosure. The zoo was packed! I had never seen so many people there. Everyone wanted to see the little pandas.

My Zoo Crew job for the day was helping at the gift shop. This was near the panda enclosure. There were so many panda toys and other panda things for sale. Everywhere you looked, there were pandas. I was very happy.

I filled the shelves with stuffed panda toys quite a few times. So many people wanted a gift. This would remind them of their first look at the cubs. Lots of people giggled when they saw my panda-painted fingernails.

Say "friend" 朋友
péngyou
(pung-yoh)

Panda Nails

How would you like to take ten tiny pandas with you wherever you go? You can! Simply paint them on your nails.

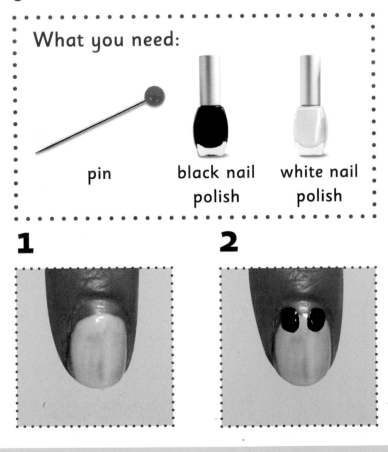

What you need:

pin

black nail polish

white nail polish

1

2

1. For each nail, paint with white polish, leaving a space at the base. Let the polish dry.
2. Use the head of a pin to make two dots for the ears with black polish.
3. Then make two dots for the eyes and one for the nose.
4. Let the polish dry. Use a pin to add tiny dots to the middle of the black eyes with white polish.

3

4

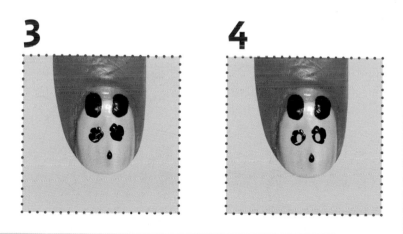

Later, I went to the panda enclosure. I wanted to see how the cubs and Zhen Mei were doing. It took a while, but I got close enough to take a look. First, I spotted Little Cloud. He was playing with some bamboo on the jungle gym. His sister was looking down on him from above. I think she was trying to escape from his teasing!

Say "goodbye"
zàijiàn
(dzi-jyen) 再见

Next, I saw Zhen Mei. She was keeping an eye on everyone. Like other parents, she wanted to keep her babies safe. Then a wonderful thing happened. Zhen Mei looked right at me, and waved!

It was the most amazing end to an exciting year. I never expected to meet a baby panda, let alone two. I never expected a panda to wave at me, either. I do expect to stick around with the Zoo Crew. Maybe I'll see you at the zoo someday.

Louise
X

Circle of Life

A panda starts having babies between the ages of 4 and 8 years.

A cub leaves its mum when it is 2 years old.

A newborn panda is pink and tiny. Black patches appear on its skin after a few days.

After a month, the baby looks like a mini grown-up panda.

At 3–4 months, the cub can stand and walk.

A panda starts eating bamboo when it is 6 months old.

The Great Panda Quiz

1. In which country do wild giant pandas live?

2. What do pandas mainly eat?

3. For how long are female pandas pregnant?

4. What were the names given to the panda cubs?

5. At what age did the pandas start walking?

Answers on page 64.

Glossary

director
person in charge

enclosure
place to keep
animals in

endangered
at risk of becoming
extinct because
numbers of that
animal are very low

habitat
place where animals
live and grow

hibernate
sleep all winter

jungle gym
structure to play
and climb on

nursery
room for babies to
sleep and play in
and be looked after

research
study to find
out more about
something

ultrasound
picture of a baby
while still inside
its mother

Guide for Parents

DK Reads is a three-level interactive reading adventure series for children, developing the habit of reading widely for both pleasure and information. These chapter books have an exciting main narrative interspersed with a range of reading genres to suit your child's reading ability, as required by the National Curriculum. Each book is designed to develop your child's reading skills, fluency, grammar awareness, and comprehension in order to build confidence and engagement when reading.

Ready for a *Starting to Read Alone* book

YOUR CHILD SHOULD

- be able to read most words without needing to stop and break them down into sound parts.
- read smoothly, in phrases and with expression. By this level, your child will be mostly reading silently.
- self-correct when some word or sentence doesn't sound right.

A VALUABLE AND SHARED READING EXPERIENCE

For some children, text reading, particularly non-fiction, requires much effort but adult participation can make this both fun and easier. So here are a few tips on how to use this book with your child.

TIP 1 Check out the contents together before your child begins:

- invite your child to check the blurb, contents page and layout of the book and comment on it.
- ask your child to make predictions about the story.
- chat about the information your child might want to find out.

TIP 2 Encourage fluent and flexible reading:

- support your child to read in fluent, expressive phrases, making full use of punctuation and thinking about the meaning.

- encourage your child to slow down and check information where appropriate.

TIP 3 Indicators that your child is reading for meaning:
- your child will be responding to the text if he/she is self-correcting and varying his/her voice.
- your child will want to chat about what he/she is reading or is eager to turn the page to find out what will happen next.

TIP 4 Praise, share and chat:
- the factual pages tend to be more difficult than the story pages, and are designed to be shared with your child.
- encourage your child to recall specific details after each chapter.
- provide opportunities for your child to pick out interesting words and discuss what they mean.
- discuss how the author captures the reader's interest, or how effective the non-fiction layouts are.
- ask questions about the text. These help to develop comprehension skills and awareness of the language used.

A FEW ADDITIONAL TIPS
- Read to your child regularly to demonstrate fluency, phrasing and expression; to find out or check information; and for sharing enjoyment.
- Encourage your child to reread favourite texts to increase reading confidence and fluency.
- Check that your child is reading a range of different types, such as poems, jokes and following instructions.

Series consultant **Shirley Bickler** is a longtime advocate of carefully crafted, enthralling texts for young readers. Her LIFT initiative for infant teaching was the model for the National Literacy Strategy Literacy Hour, and she is co-author of *Book Bands for Guided Reading* published by Reading Recovery based at the Institute of Education.

Index

Answers to the Great Panda Quiz:

1. China; 2. Bamboo; 3. Three to five
months; 4. Snowdrop, Little Cloud;
5. Around four months.